CONTENTS

KU-352-045

CHAPTER 1

AN EXCITING
Landing

A spacecraft zoomed through space. It had travelled millions of miles. The trip took almost nine months. On 6 August 2012, the spacecraft reached Mars.

Then it prepared to land a robot called

a **rover**. The rover was named *Curiosity*.

Curiosity left Earth on
26 November 2011.

GETTING TO MARS

People waited for good news about *Curiosity*. **NASA engineers** watched their computers.

Other objects had landed on Mars. But none were as big as *Curiosity*. It was the size of a car!

Landing the rover would be hard. Something might go wrong. It could crash!

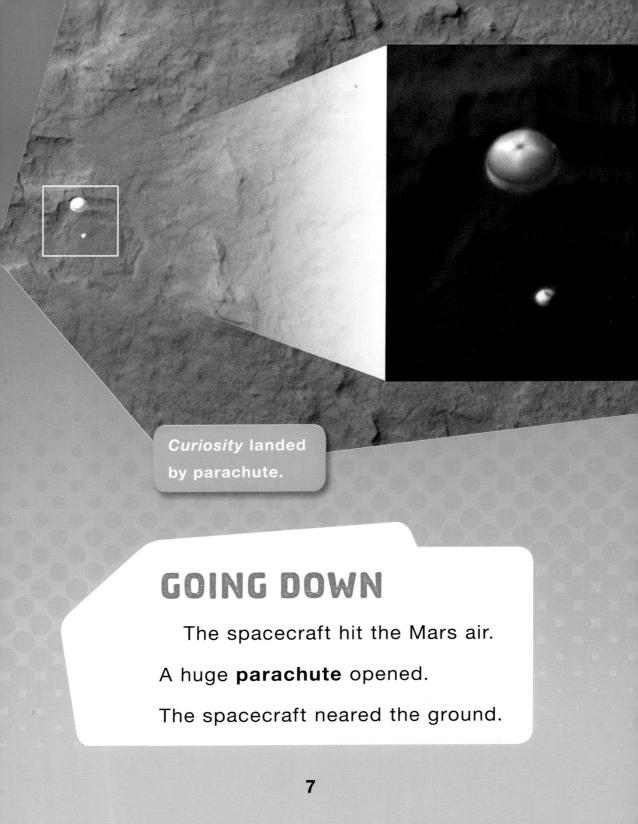

Curiosity landed by parachute.

GOING DOWN

The spacecraft hit the Mars air.

A huge **parachute** opened.

The spacecraft neared the ground.

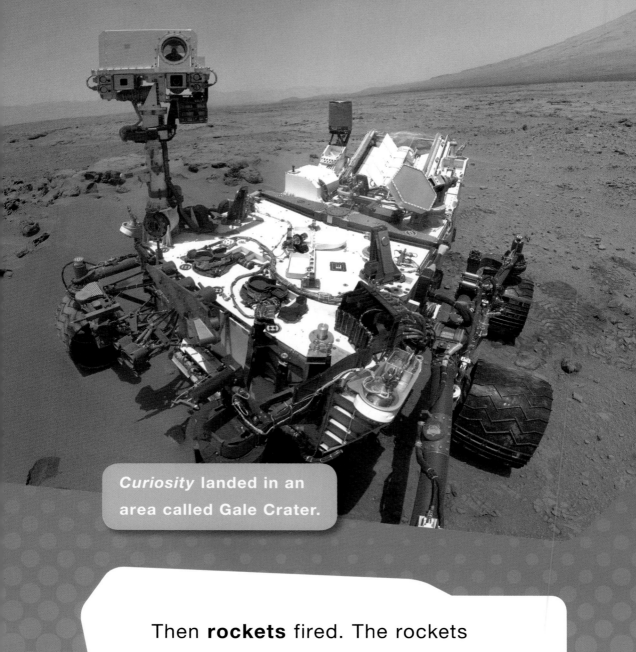

Curiosity landed in an area called Gale Crater.

Then **rockets** fired. The rockets slowed the spacecraft. It hung in the air.

Next came the tricky part. The spacecraft stayed in the air. It lowered *Curiosity* on a huge rope. It set the rover down gently.

Curiosity was safe on the surface. Everyone at NASA cheered!

ROVER TOOLS

Curiosity has many cameras. Its tools test rocks and soil. The rover also records the weather.

CHAPTER 2

THE RED Planet

Mars is a cold planet. Its surface is rocks and dust. Some areas look like dry rivers. There might have been life once. **Scientists** wanted to take a closer look.

Mars is the fourth
planet from the Sun.

REACHING MARS

Landing on Mars would not be easy. Rovers leave Earth on rockets. The rockets shake and rattle them.

In space, there are dangers. The trip to Mars is long and cold. Sometimes the Sun gives off bursts of power. These can damage machines.

Giant rockets start Mars rovers on their journeys.

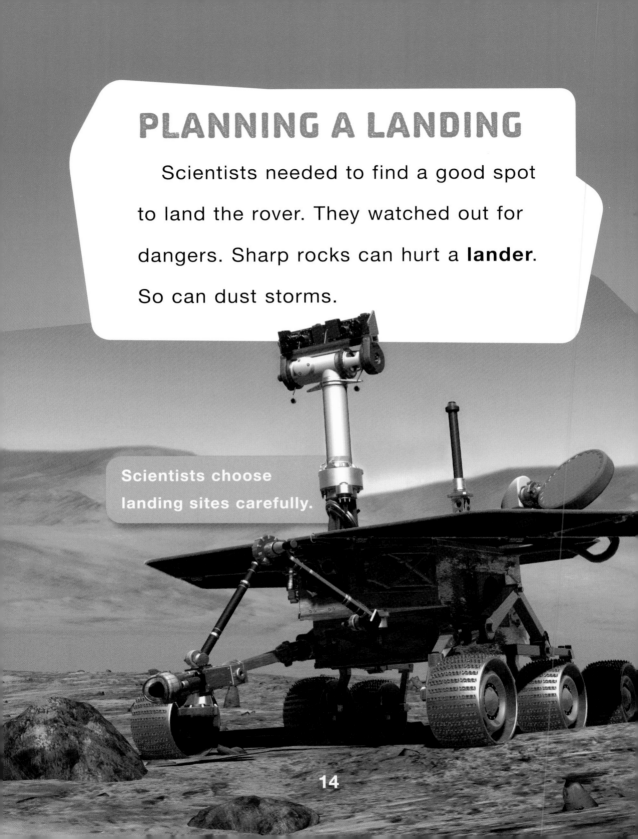

PLANNING A LANDING

Scientists needed to find a good spot to land the rover. They watched out for dangers. Sharp rocks can hurt a **lander**. So can dust storms.

Scientists choose landing sites carefully.

14

RED MARS

Mars's red colour comes from iron in its soil.

Spacecraft travel very fast towards Mars. The air on Mars is thin. It doesn't slow down a lander very well. Engineers studied how to land safely.

CHAPTER 3

MISSIONS TO Mars

NASA's first success on Mars came in 1976. Two landers arrived. They were called *Viking 1* and *Viking 2*.

The landers used parachutes. Then they fired rockets. This slowed them down. They touched down on three legs.

Viking 1 worked on Mars for six years. *Viking 2* worked for four years. They sent data to Earth. But they couldn't move around.

Viking landers looked for signs of life on Mars.

Spirit's lander floated to the surface.

A NEW PATH ON MARS

In 1997, people made a new kind of lander. The Pathfinder **mission** sent the first Mars rover. The rover could move around on the surface.

Pathfinder had a parachute and rockets. It also had airbags. These gave it a soft landing. The rover rolled off the lander.

Two other rovers landed in 2004. They were named *Spirit* and *Opportunity*. Both used airbags to land.

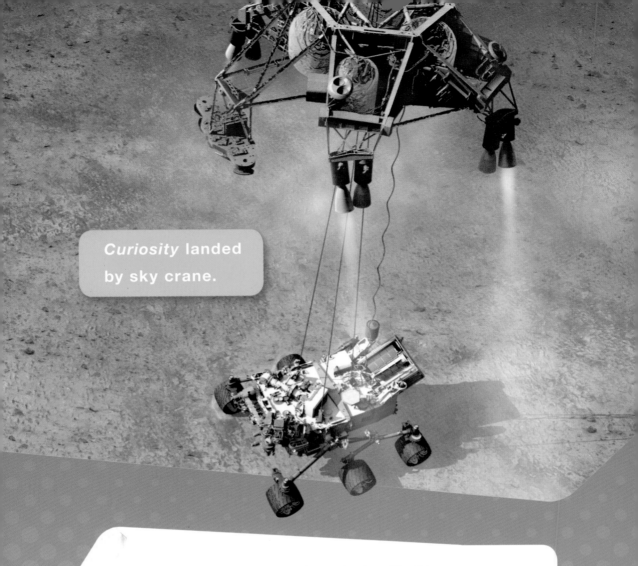

Curiosity landed by sky crane.

CURIOSITY LANDS

Curiosity brought new problems. It was much bigger than earlier rovers. Airbags wouldn't work.

Scientists needed to find a new way to land the rover. Helicopters gave them an idea. Helicopters hover. Then they drop **cargo**.

Scientists created a sky **crane**. This Mars spacecraft hovered. It lowered *Curiosity*. Then the spacecraft let go. *Curiosity* landed safely.

NEAR MISSES

The Soviet Union crashed two landers in 1971. One worked for just 20 seconds before breaking.

CHAPTER 4

MARS OF Tomorrow

Landers help people study Mars. Scientists learn about its weather, soil and rocks. One lander found ice. It saw snow in the air!

The *Phoenix* Mars lander discovered snow falling on Mars.

PEOPLE ON MARS?

People have walked on the Moon. One day people might walk on Mars.

A spacecraft will have to keep **astronauts** safe. It must carry food and air.

Scientists are planning new ways to land on Mars.

DANGERS ON MARS

Mars is dangerous. The planet is very cold. People can't breathe in the air. People will need spacesuits to explore.

Engineers need to find new ways to land on Mars. *Curiosity* was big. Landers with astronauts will be even bigger.

Rovers never return to Earth. But astronauts will need a way to land on Mars then leave again. Engineers are working on these problems.

A CITY ON MARS

One day people may do more than visit. They may stay on Mars. People would use water found on Mars. They would grow food in the soil.

For now, NASA will send more landers to Mars. Some old ones still work too. They still make discoveries. These discoveries help scientists plan future visits to Mars.

The *Mars 2020* rover will help scientists prepare for humans living on Mars.

GLOSSARY

astronaut
a person who goes to space

cargo
goods carried by aircraft, ship or motor vehicle

crane
a machine that lifts or lowers heavy objects

engineer
a person who plans and makes machines or buildings

lander
a spacecraft that lands on a planet or other space object such as a moon

mission
a trip into space for a purpose

NASA
the National Aeronautics and Space Administration, a US government organization

parachute
a large piece of cloth that fills with air to slow the fall of something tied to it

rocket
an engine that uses flames to move a spacecraft

rover
a robot that drives over the ground of a planet or other space object

scientist
a person who studies the world around us

Soviet Union
a former group of 15 republics that included Russia, the Ukraine and other nations in eastern Europe and northern Asia

TRIVIA

1. In 1966, the first human-made object landed on the Moon. First, rockets slowed a ship. As the ship crashed, it threw the lander into the air. The lander then bounced on airbags.

2. Venus is the second planet from the Sun. In 1970, a lander touched down on Venus. The thick air and a parachute helped slow the lander. Landers don't last long on Venus. It is blazing hot! No landers have been sent to Venus since 1984.

3. The Rosetta mission reached a comet in 2014. A lander touched down. Its legs took the force of the fall. The legs of the lander should have dug into the comet with screws. But the screws failed. The comet was too hard. The lander bounced to a stop instead. The Rosetta mission ended in 2016.

ACTIVITY

LANDING AN EGG

Ask an adult before doing this activity. Find an egg. This is your lander! If you hold out your hand and drop it, the egg will probably break. Try to drop it so it doesn't crack. Use balloons, paper, a box or anything else you want. Try your idea with a small rock first.

Did it work? Why or why not? Could you try something different? How can you safely land your egg?

FIND OUT MORE

Books

Astronaut in Training (Raintree, 2017), Kathryn Clay

Exploring Mars: An Interactive Space Exploration Adventure (You Choose), Steve Kortenkamp (Raintree, 2016)

Mars Rovers (Space Tech), Allan Morey (Epic Books, 2017)

Welcome to Mars: Making a Home on the Red Planet (Science & Nature), Buzz Aldrin (National Geographic Kids, 2015)

Websites

Mars information for children by NASA:
   mars.nasa.gov/participate/funzone/

Solar system exploration for children by NASA:
   solarsystem.nasa.gov/kids/do-it-yourself/

INDEX

Raintree is an imprint of Capstone Global Library Limited, a company incorporated in England and Wales having its registered office at 264 Banbury Road, Oxford, OX2 7DY – Registered company number: 6695582

www.raintree.co.uk
myorders@raintree.co.uk

Editor: Megan Gunderson
Designer: Becky Daum
Production Specialist: Dan Peluso
Originated by Capstone Global Library Limited
Printed and bound in India

ISBN 978 1 4747 7525 0 (hardback)
22 21 20 19 18
10 9 8 7 6 5 4 3 2 1

ISBN 978 1 4747 7349 2 (paperback)
23 22 21 20 19
10 9 8 7 6 5 4 3 2 1

British Library Cataloguing in Publication Data
A full catalogue record for this book is available from the British Library.

Acknowledgements
AP Images: Terry Renna, 5; iStockphoto: serts, 31 (background); NASA, 10–11, 12–13, 14–15, JPL, 17, JPL-Caltech, cover (foreground), 20–21, 26–27, JPL-Caltech/Malin Space Science Systems, 8–9, JPL-Caltech/UA/Lockheed Martin, 22–23, JPL-Caltech/Univ. of Arizona, 6–7; Science Source: Detlev van Ravenswaay, 18–19; Shutterstock Images: albumkoretsky, 31 (parachute), Nattika, 30, 31 (egg), sandystifler, cover (background); SpaceX: 24–25.
Design Elements: iStockphoto, Red Line Editorial, and Shutterstock Images

We would like to thank Professor Jim Bell at the School of Earth and Space Exploration, Arizona State University, for his invaluable help in the preparation of this book.

Every effort has been made to contact copyright holders of material reproduced in this book. Any omissions will be rectified in subsequent printings if notice is given to the publisher.

All the internet addresses (URLs) given in this book were valid at the time of going to press. However, due to the dynamic nature of the internet, some addresses may have changed, or sites may have changed or ceased to exist since publication. While the author and publisher regret any inconvenience this may cause readers, no responsibility for any such changes can be accepted by either the author or the publisher.

BRIGHT IDEA BOOKS

HOW DID
Robots
LAND ON
MARS?

Clara MacCarald

raintree